THROUGH THE EYES OF FORMULA 1

PERSONAL IMAGES AND INSIGHTS FROM THE STARS OF F1 RACING

1

PUBLISHED BY

Dennis Publishing Limited

30 Cleveland Street, London W1T 4JD

Publishing director: Geoff Love
Editorial: Caroline Reid, Christian Sylt
Design: Mark Sommer
Production: Dan McCalla
Artwork: Tracey Radnall

Repro: Gildenburgh Ltd, 30 Stapledon Road,
Orton Southgate, Peterborough PE2 6TD
Printed by: Butler Tanner & Dennis, Caxton
Road, Frome, Somerset BA11 1NF
Distributed by: Pan Macmillan,
20 New Wharf Road, London N1 9RR

Group managing director: Ian Westwood
Chief financial officer: Brett Reynolds
Group finance director: Ian Leggett
CEO: James Tye
Chairman: Felix Dennis

CONTENTS

3

FOREWORD

FORMULA 1 IS the world's most watched annual sport and its drivers are known the world over. Every move they make on track is watched by millions but very few people ever get a glimpse into their lives when they aren't racing. It leaves fans guessing about the pets the drivers have, where they go on holiday and the hobbies they get up to on weekends off.

This book gives a taste of what the lives of the F1 drivers and team principals are really like. Each of them has taken a photograph of anything they wanted and they are all printed on the following pages. They are views that no-one else could get and they show the drivers' pets, their toys and favourite places. There are even photos taken from the driver's seat of an F1 car sitting in the pit lane and through the living room window of a team principal's holiday home.

It has been done for a wonderful cause because the sale of this book will benefit Great Ormond Street Hospital Children's Charity and all the photos have been signed and sold at an auction in aid of it.

The F1 Group has been supporting Great Ormond Street Hospital for many years and we are proud to be able to help with the tremendous work they do. Every year the hospital treats nearly 200,000 sick children and by buying this book you are helping them keep it up. You are also getting a glimpse into a side of F1 that isn't shown on television and as you will see, it isn't all about fast cars and champagne.

BERNIE ECCLESTONE, SEPTEMBER 2012

ABOUT ZOOM

ZOOM started with a very simple idea. Christian Sylt and Caroline Reid, authors of Formula 1's industry monitor *Formula Money*, realised that although there are many charity auctions in sport, they all tend to follow a similar pattern. The items on offer are usually signed photos of the athletes or the kit that they use. They often raise a great deal of money but despite carrying an autograph, the items tell the buyer little new about the star who signed them. Zoom was set up to rectify that by turning the tables and asking all the drivers and team principals in F1 to take photographs which would then be signed and put up for auction.

Never before has there been an auction of signed photos taken by the stars of any sport and several things were crucial to making it happen. The first was gaining support from the world-renowned Great Ormond Street Hospital, which has a long association with F1. It loved the unique concept behind Zoom and was chosen to receive the proceeds from the auction. Next, top motoring auction house Coys agreed to handle the sale and Influence, F1's leading communications and marketing firm, became a partner in Zoom alongside *Formula Money*.

One of the most important steps in establishing Zoom was the final one and this was getting the support of F1's chief executive Bernie Ecclestone, who Christian has known for a decade. Bernie's support has been invaluable and the participation of all the drivers and team principals soon followed. Such has been the level of interest in Zoom that several former F1 drivers, champions, commentators and designers have also agreed to take part.

All the photographers took to the challenge with gusto. We never expected to get such a diverse group of photos showing both insider views from the track and personal pictures which have nothing to do with racing. Who would have thought that a picture of a rusty old tractor would be close to the heart of Adrian Newey, a man who is famous for the sleek high-tech cars he designs so successfully? Likewise, Russian driver Vitaly Petrov's photo of a giant earth-mover came as a surprise, as did Sebastian Vettel's mountain vista and the two statues taken by Bernie. This collection of photos doesn't just give a glimpse into the lives of F1's superstars – it reveals what drives them.

Zoom is on track to become an annual project so it can help a wonderful cause on a regular basis. All the F1 teams, team bosses and drivers have played a key part in making this happen and we sincerely thank them along with everyone else who has donated a photo. We would also like to thank Zoom's partners: Coys, the Wyndham Grand London Chelsea Harbour, TAG Heuer, Kingfisher, Barbarella, Memento Exclusives, Sutton Images, ID PR's Alison Hill and Christine Gorham from RKM Communications.

Special thanks also need to go to Bernie, and to Great Ormond Street Hospital Children's Charity – we are proud to be a part of helping them continue with the tremendous work they do.

CAROLINE REID AND CHRISTIAN SYLT,
SEPTEMBER 2012

SEBASTIAN VETTEL

TEAM RED BULL RACING | **DATE OF BIRTH** 03/07/1987 | **NATIONALITY** GERMAN

Sebastian Vettel only turned 25 in 2012 but is already one of the most decorated drivers in the history of the sport. On his debut with BMW in 2007, he became the youngest driver ever to score a point at 19, and by 21 he'd become the youngest driver to win a race with victory at the 2008 Italian Grand Prix for Toro Rosso. He switched to Red Bull Racing for 2009 when he finished second in the championship and followed it up with two world titles in 2010 and 2011 - making him the youngest double champion. He also holds the record for the most pole positions in a season at 15 (set in 2011) and is also the fastest driver among the F1 stars to attempt *Top Gear*'s Star In A Reasonably-Priced Car challenge.

THE RED WALL MOUNTAIN

"This mountain in Vorarlberg in Austria is known as the Red Wall. I love it – it's such an awesome view! I know the area really well; I went on my first skiing trip there with my family and my good friend Joschi Walch, who ran the hospitality unit when I made my F1 debut [for BMW] and now has a hotel in the area. I love to go to the region on holiday and it really is a home away from home – F1 catering boss Karl-Heinz Zimmermann also has his restaurant nearby."

MARK WEBBER

TEAM RED BULL RACING | **DATE OF BIRTH** 27/08/1976 | **NATIONALITY** AUSTRALIAN

Mark Webber showed his star potential right from the start of his F1 career, scoring a miraculous fifth place on his debut at the 2002 Australian Grand Prix, racing a Minardi car in which it was often an achievement just to qualify. After a few years in cars that didn't match his talent, the Australian joined Red Bull Racing in 2007 but was initially hit by more reliability woes and disappointment. After 130 races, he finally scored his first victory at the 2009 German Grand Prix and hasn't looked back since.

SIMBA AND SHADOW STOP FOR A DRINK ON A LONG WALK

"All us drivers know how much we love hotels but it's always good to be at home. The best thing about going home to my dogs, Simba and Shadow, is that they don't know if I've had a bad day or a good day but they're always happy to see me. I live in England and even though I love racing everywhere, there is that extra little something at Silverstone that makes you a bit more relaxed and a bit more comfortable."

JENSON BUTTON

TEAM McLAREN | **DATE OF BIRTH** 19/01/1980 | **NATIONALITY** BRITISH

Jenson Button's F1 career has been a rollercoaster ride. Hailed as a great talent on his debut for Williams in 2000, he spent several years in the wilderness as he constantly seemed to be driving for the wrong team at the wrong time. Despite his obvious talent, he contested 113 races before chalking up his first win, at the chaotic wet Hungarian Grand Prix in 2006 for Honda, but the team's performance plummeted almost immediately thereafter and for the next couple of seasons it was a struggle for him just to score points. Honda pulled its backing of the team for 2009, but against all odds Button was rewarded for his patience with an unexpected world championship as the squad, renamed Brawn, soldiered on through the year. Button has since switched to McLaren where he has continued his race-winning form.

VIEW OF THE PIT WALL

"They gave me a camera and this was the first thing I saw, so I thought it'd be funny to get a shot of Martin [Whitmarsh, McLaren team principal]. I'm not sure if he's looking at me with a smile or a smirk! We have a lot of fun together and I wanted to take him a bit by surprise. This picture tells you a lot about where we work – it's the end of a practice session at Spa-Francorchamps, so what you see here is very much the average working day of a Formula 1 driver."

13

LEWIS HAMILTON

TEAM McLAREN | **DATE OF BIRTH** 07/01/1985 | **NATIONALITY** BRITISH

Lewis Hamilton's path to F1 was mapped out early. At the age of just 13, his winning performances in karting drew the attention of McLaren founder Ron Dennis, who was so impressed that he signed the youngster up to McLaren's junior driver programme, including an option that if Hamilton ever made it to F1, McLaren would get first refusal on his services. Nine years later, Hamilton made his F1 debut in a McLaren and the following season, he became the youngest-ever world champion (at the time) in a thrilling last-lap conclusion to the 2008 season.

IN THE COCKPIT AT THE BELGIAN GRAND PRIX

"Welcome to my office! I thought it would be nice to get a shot of the view from the cockpit of my car. It's always a pretty amazing view – I still never get used to being in a Formula 1 car. Here I wanted to capture the fact that while it's very cramped inside the car and there's a lot of action going on all around me, it's the place where I feel more comfortable than anywhere else. It's more like a second home than your office. The gloves on the wheel are like leaving your boots on the mat – a sign of being at home."

15

FERNANDO ALONSO

TEAM FERRARI | **DATE OF BIRTH** 29/07/1981 | **NATIONALITY** SPANISH

Fernando Alonso is now known as one of the most successful drivers in F1, but it wasn't always an easy ride. He started his F1 career in 2001 driving for Minardi, a team synonymous with failure, but he still managed to impress the sport's power brokers. For 2003 he landed a race drive with Renault and took his first victory at the Hungarian Grand Prix. World championships followed in 2005 and 2006, making him one of an elite group to win back-to-back titles. Alonso made the switch to Ferrari in 2010, bringing together two of the biggest names in Formula 1.

FELIPE MASSA AT FERRARI'S *WROOOM* PRESS EVENT

"Events like these are special because, for once, they allow you to spend time together away from the frenetic pace of the track and the working environment of the factory. It's a nice way to get to know one another better and to find the sort of understanding you get with a second family. I think these events are part of what makes Ferrari a special team, different from all the others."

17

FELIPE MASSA

TEAM FERRARI | **DATE OF BIRTH** 25/04/1981 | **NATIONALITY** BRAZILIAN

Felipe Massa's F1 career has been dominated by two unlucky incidents. The first came in the final round of the 2008 championship at his home race, the Brazilian Grand Prix. Massa took the chequered flag for victory and it seemed to everyone that he had also won the championship. However, in the rain behind him, Timo Glock ran wide at the last corner, allowing title rival Lewis Hamilton to gain one place and snatch the championship by a single point. Then, just months later, Massa was seriously injured when a stray suspension spring from another car burst through his visor at the 2009 Hungarian GP. He returned to F1 the following year and remains one of the most popular drivers on the grid.

ROB SMEDLEY AND 'GIANT FELIPE'

"Rob can be my engineer, he can be my psychologist, he can be my friend. I know everything about him and he knows everything about me. But he doesn't see me as an Formula 1 driver like a lot of other people, who might be afraid about what they should do or say to me."

MICHAEL SCHUMACHER

TEAM MERCEDES | **DATE OF BIRTH** 03/01/1969 | **NATIONALITY** GERMAN

2012 FORMULA 1 SHEL

Michael Schumacher is the most successful driver in Formula 1 history, with an unsurpassed seven world titles – two with Benetton and five for Ferrari – and a string of records including most wins, most pole positions and the highest number of race wins in a single season (13 in 2004). He initially retired from F1 in 2006, but the lure of racing at the top level proved too much for him to resist and he returned in 2010 with the revived Mercedes team.

FROM THE COCKPIT AT SUZUKA

"If I had to find a title for this picture, it would simply be 'the office'. The cockpit of a Formula 1 car is a place where I feel completely at home, and everything is second nature. The experience is even more enjoyable at a driver's circuit like Suzuka in Japan, where you constantly have to challenge yourself and the car to go right to the limits."

NICO ROSBERG

TEAM MERCEDES | **DATE OF BIRTH** 27/06/1985 | **NATIONALITY** GERMAN

Nico Rosberg's father Keke was Formula One world champion in 1982 and the junior Rosberg made his own F1 debut in 2006 driving for his dad's old team, Williams. From the start he showed he had inherited some of his father's skill and at his first race he became the youngest driver ever to set a fastest lap. He regularly featured in the points and scored his first podium with the team at the 2008 Australian Grand Prix. For 2010 he moved to the revived works Mercedes team which brought him regular podium places and at the 2012 Chinese GP he took his first victory, the first for Mercedes since Juan Manuel Fangio won the 1955 Italian GP.

GRID GIRL IN SINGAPORE

"Singapore is one of my favourite races. I love the atmosphere there and that's why I have chosen this picture. It was taken when we go to the driver's parade with all the classic cars. Here you can see my driver already waiting for me and the beautiful grid girl – on the starting grid you don't notice these things because there are so many things to do just before starting the race. You can also see the Singapore Flyer at the back. It's always special when the race starts in the light and then gets dark when the night comes, and Singapore has become like a second Monaco in the calendar. I have a good friend living in Singapore and so I like visiting very much. I always spend more than a week in this amazing city."

23

KIMI RÄIKKÖNEN

TEAM LOTUS | **DATE OF BIRTH** 17/10/1979 | **NATIONALITY** FINNISH

Kimi Räikkönen, known as the 'Iceman', stunned the motorsport world when he was given his debut F1 drive with Sauber in 2001. The Finn had previously competed in just 23 car races at junior levels, although he had won more than half of them. Despite his doubters he took sixth place in his first race and by 2003 claimed his first victory at the wheel of a McLaren, finishing second in that year's championship. He switched to Ferrari for 2007, winning the championship at the final race, but when the results dried up he sensationally quit F1 at the end of 2009. He turned to the World Rally Championship instead, but couldn't replicate his F1 success and by 2012 he was back in F1 in a Lotus, with a string of good results proving he hadn't lost his touch.

BLACK, GOLD AND RED

"I was about to go to the track on Friday in Melbourne earlier this year for my first drive of the season, to officially become an F1 driver again after two years away. There are black, red and gold reflections in the picture, which reminded me of my new team."

25

ROMAIN GROSJEAN

TEAM LOTUS | **DATE OF BIRTH** 17/04/1986 | **NATIONALITY** FRENCH

Romain Grosjean got his first taste of F1 in 2009, when he was drafted into the Renault team for seven races. The best result he managed was a 13th place and he wasn't retained for 2010. He returned to the GP2 junior series, taking the 2011 championship, by which time he was back as a F1 test driver with his old team. Few people seriously expected he would get another proper shot at F1 and there was widespread surprise when he was signed as a race driver for 2012 with Renault, by now renamed Lotus. The surprise turned to shock as Grosjean delivered one stunning performance after another, making him a firm fan favourite and establishing him as a future star of the sport.

BALLOONS IN MELBOURNE

"Sunday morning in Melbourne: I was about to contest my first race with Lotus and we had managed to take third position on the grid the day before. When I opened the curtains on race day, I saw these hot air balloons in the sky and captured what was a very special moment."

PAUL DI RESTA

TEAM FORCE INDIA | **DATE OF BIRTH** 16/04/1986 | **NATIONALITY** BRITISH

Paul di Resta comes from a racing family. Three-time Indianapolis 500 winner Dario Franchitti is his cousin and there are other racers in the family, although di Resta is the first to make it into Formula 1. He had a successful pre-F1 career, winning the Formula 3 Euroseries and DTM titles, before joining Force India in 2011. Since then he has secured several good points finishes and has been tipped as a future Grand Prix winner.

ON THE GRID AT THE ITALIAN GRAND PRIX

"This photo shows my car on the grid at Monza in 2011, a few minutes before the start of the race. It shows how busy it can be on the grid and how much equipment the team needs to prepare the cars for the start. It's the time when you have your final chat with the engineers and just try to focus on the race ahead."

29

NICO HÜLKENBERG

TEAM FORCE INDIA | **DATE OF BIRTH** 19/08/1987 | **NATIONALITY** GERMAN

Nico Hülkenberg made his Formula 1 debut for Williams in 2010 and gained several points finishes, as well as a stunning pole position at the Brazilian Grand Prix, in a car that was far from the class of the field. However, Hülkenberg was dropped for 2011 as Williams required drivers to bring in sponsorship as well as points. He joined Force India as test driver and was rewarded with a race seat for 2012. He regularly featured in the top ten and scored a career best of fourth place at the Belgian GP.

ART CAR

"This is quite a special car - the first Formula 1 art car, created by Dexter Brown. I went to do a PR event with the team before the car was auctioned for charity. I like the colours of the car and it's unusual for a Formula 1 car to become a piece of art."

KAMUI KOBAYASHI

TEAM SAUBER | **DATE OF BIRTH** 13/09/1986 | **NATIONALITY** JAPANESE

Kamui Kobayashi made his F1 debut with Toyota at the 2009 Japanese Grand Prix as a replacement for the injured Timo Glock. To the surprise of many, he fought with world championship leader Jenson Button for position and held him off for several laps, Button jokingly describing him as "absolutely crazy". When Toyota quit the sport at the end of that season, he was snapped up by Sauber where he has been widely praised for his aggressive style and overtaking ability.

MOUNT FUJI

"I took this picture when I visited Mount Fuji for the first time. The Japanese Alps provide a beautiful landscape. You can go a long way up this holy mountain by car and this view is what you see when this road ends."

SERGIO PÉREZ

TEAM SAUBER | **DATE OF BIRTH** 26/01/1990 | **NATIONALITY** MEXICAN

Sergio Pérez was hailed as a star of the future when he moved into F1 in 2011 with Sauber and so far has not disappointed. The talented Mexican took multiple points finishes in his first season in F1, but his second turned out even better. At the second race of the season, the Malaysian Grand Prix, he finished second and for a time even looked like he might overtake Fernando Alonso's Ferrari for victory. Another podium followed at the Canadian Grand Prix, where Perez finished third from 15th on the grid.

CANELO, MY DOG

"This is my dog Canelo. I really like him a lot and I have had him for two years. Unfortunately I don't get to see him very often as he lives with my family in Guadalajara and I'm travelling most of the year. But he is always the first one I greet when I come back to my home town in Mexico."

DANIEL RICCIARDO

TEAM TORO ROSSO | **DATE OF BIRTH** 01/07/1989 | **NATIONALITY** AUSTRALIAN

Daniel Ricciardo made his mark on the road to F1 by emulating many of the greats in winning the prestigious British Formula Three championship in 2009. It caught the eye of Formula 1 bosses and he was appointed as Toro Rosso's test driver for 2010. The team saw him as a future star and placed him in a race drive at HRT for the second half of 2011, where he impressed with some solid drives. Toro Rosso promoted him to a race seat for 2012 and he scored points on his debut at his home race, the Australian Grand Prix.

QUAD BIKING IN AUSTRALIA

"Quad biking is awesome! There's a lot of great beaches near my home town of Perth that are ideal for it – I love heading up to Lancelin or further north to Jurien Bay. Camping and quad biking with friends is a perfect weekend for me, although putting my feet up and having a couple of cold beers never hurt."

JEAN-ERIC VERGNE

TEAM TORO ROSSO | **DATE OF BIRTH** 25/04/1990 | **NATIONALITY** FRENCH

Jean-Eric Vergne established his reputation in British Formula Three, winning the 2010 championship with 13 race victories. He was appointed as a test driver for Toro Rosso in 2011, continuing his Red Bull partnership. This evolved into a race drive for 2012 and he made his debut at the season opener, the Australian Grand Prix. He just missed out on a points finish, but scored at the following race in Malaysia and picked up more points at the Belgian GP later in the year.

IN THE TEAM PRINCIPAL'S OFFICE

"As a racing driver, you rely on the support of a lot of people who work very hard to give you a good car and to put you in the best possible situation for every race. There are the mechanics who actually put everything together, your race engineer who helps you make the car go faster and then, overseeing it all, is the team principal. Ultimately everything is down to him. At the track, most team bosses have their office in the team hospitality area, but Franz Tost always likes to be at the heart of the action. Here he is in his office behind the garage, next to the engineers' meeting room."

39

PASTOR MALDONADO

TEAM WILLIAMS | **DATE OF BIRTH** 10/03/1985 | **NATIONALITY** VENEZUELAN

When Pastor Maldonado first entered F1 with Williams in 2011, there were many observers who doubted he was good enough to cut it at the top level. He brought substantial sponsorship from Venezuelan oil company PDVSA with him and this was believed to be instrumental in Williams's decision to sign him rather than keep its existing driver line-up. However, all that was put behind him when he surged to victory in the 2012 Spanish Grand Prix, securing Williams's first win in nearly eight years and making him the first Venezuelan to top a Grand Prix podium.

SAPO FALLS

"This picture is of the Sapo Falls (also known as Frog Falls) in the Canaima National Park in Venezuela. I am a proud Venezuelan and it is a beautiful country, something this photo clearly shows."

BRUNO SENNA

TEAM WILLIAMS | **DATE OF BIRTH** 15/10/1983 | **NATIONALITY** BRAZILIAN

As the nephew of the legendary triple world champion Ayrton Senna, Bruno's first taste of F1 came from his uncle, who taught him the tricks of the trade. When Ayrton was tragically killed on track in 1994, Bruno's mother discouraged him from a racing career, but the Brazilian still loved racing and at 21, ditched his studies for a business degree and headed off to England to follow in his uncle's footsteps. He made his F1 debut for HRT in 2010, scored his first points a year later for Renault and in 2012 signed for Ayrton's former team Williams.

ON THE BEACH

"This photograph is of my family's beach house just south of Rio in Brazil. I have many happy memories of this house, spending a lot of time here as a child surrounded by my family. It has breathtaking scenery and is very tranquil so I like to visit as often as I can."

43

HEIKKI KOVALAINEN

TEAM CATERHAM | **DATE OF BIRTH** 19/10/1981 | **NATIONALITY** FINNISH

Heikki Kovalainen spent a season driving for Renault before he got his big break driving for McLaren in 2008, filling the vacancy created when Fernando Alonso quit the team. Following in the footsteps of Finnish world champions Keke Rosberg, Mika Häkkinen and Kimi Räikkönen, Kovalainen showed talent of his own when he won the Hungarian Grand Prix that year. The 2009 season was more difficult, however, and after failing to score a podium he left the end of the year to join the fledgling Lotus team. The new team was not a match for the established outfits and didn't score a point, though Kovalainen helped it outpace the other two newcomers on the grid. The Finn is also known for his love of golf and witty Twitter feed.

INSIDE THE DRIVER ROOM

"This is my driver's room in the Caterham F1 Team motorhome at the track. I have a pretty intense schedule at every Grand Prix and this is the only place where I can really be on my own and relax during a race weekend. I prepare for every session on track in here with my physio and when I have a few minutes to myself, I switch on the PlayStation and play a bit of golf."

VITALY PETROV

TEAM CATERHAM | **DATE OF BIRTH** 08/09/1984 | **NATIONALITY** RUSSIAN

Russia's first ever Formula 1 driver was an unlikely candidate to become a top racing driver. At more than 6ft, he is taller than most of the grid and unlike his rivals he never competed in karting, starting instead in ice races in his homeland. This unusual background didn't prevent him from making his mark when he moved into single-seater racing, winning four GP2 races before he entered F1 with Renault in 2010. His first season brought patchy results, but he put in a strong performance at the 2011 season opener in Melbourne to take third place ahead of Fernando Alonso, Mark Webber and Jenson Button. He switched to Caterham for 2012.

F1 TRACK CONSTRUCTION IN SOCHI

"Every driver looks forward to racing in his home country, but so far I've not had the opportunity. I took this photo of a giant digger at the circuit in Sochi, which is under construction and will host the very first Russian Grand Prix in 2014. I'm very proud that my country has made this decision. F1 is getting more popular in Russia all the time and I'm really looking forward to racing in front of my home crowd. It will be a very special feeling."

PEDRO DE LA ROSA

TEAM HRT | **DATE OF BIRTH** 24/02/1971 | **NATIONALITY** SPANISH

Pedro de la Rosa is one of the most experienced drivers on the Formula 1 grid. He made his debut for the Arrows team in 1999, scoring a sixth place on his debut, and was snapped up by Jaguar for 2001. However, points were hard to come by despite the prestigious name, and de la Rosa moved to McLaren as a test driver for 2003. He became one of the team's race drivers in 2006 when Juan Pablo Montoya suddenly quit F1, and de la Rosa scored his first and only podium at that year's Hungarian Grand Prix before moving back to a testing role. He returned to racing for Sauber in 2010 and now drives for HRT.

LIGHTHOUSE IN MALLORCA

"For me this picture is very special because it is the entrance to the bay of Porto Colom in Mallorca, where I spend my summers. In the photo you can see the lighthouse of Porto Colom and the bow of my boat. The house on the left is the house my parents rented in summers when I was small and, as a result of spending my summers there, we decided to build our own house nearby. So this photo is special for three reasons: it has my boat, which I spend a lot of time on; the lighthouse, which is an emblem of Porto Colom; and the house we rented, which sparked our love of the area. If I were to describe in one word what I feel when looking at this picture it would be happiness because that is where I would go for a swim with my friends when I was a kid."

49

NARAIN KARTHIKEYAN

TEAM HRT | **DATE OF BIRTH** 14/01/1977 | **NATIONALITY** INDIAN

Nicknamed 'the fastest Indian in the world', Narain Karthikeyan had the weight of a nation's expectations on his shoulders when he made his F1 debut in 2005 with the Jordan team, but with only one points-scoring finish, Karthikeyan quit the team when it changed ownership at the end of the season. He found work as an F1 test driver with Williams and eventually turned his attention to other major racing series, competing in Le Mans, A1GP and NASCAR, where he was named the most popular driver in the Camping World Truck Series. With the inaugural Indian Grand Prix on the calendar for 2011, Karthikeyan was once again hot property in F1 and he switched back to the series at the wheel of a HRT.

MONTE CARLO HARBOUR

"Monaco is very special as a place, and not just because of the Grand Prix. You aspire to be in Monaco because in a way that means you have made it and this photo explains how beautiful it is. This is on a non-race day – it turns into a completely different animal once the cars get going."

TIMO GLOCK

TEAM MARUSSIA | **DATE OF BIRTH** 18/03/1982 | **NATIONALITY** GERMAN

Timo Glock made his F1 debut back in 2004 as a stand-in at the Jordan team and scored points in his very first race. He switched to ChampCar racing in the US and then GP2, before he returned to F1 with Toyota in 2008, finishing the season a credible tenth in the championship. The next year brought two podium places, including a second place in Singapore, but Toyota quit the sport at season's end and he switched to newcomer Virgin for 2010. Glock impressed with his driving but the new team struggled with reliability issues. He stayed on with the team when it became Marussia in 2012.

SINGAPORE SKYLINE

"For me this picture evokes the very special feeling we get from the Singapore Grand Prix. It is the only night race in the F1 season which, combined with the fact that it is a street race, gives it a very special atmosphere that is evident on this photograph. It is great fun to race there every time and a very special feeling to drive in the city at night. I wish that one day all our fans have the opportunity to experience this race and support the Marussia F1 Team from the grandstands there because it really is quite something."

CHARLES PIC

TEAM MARUSSIA | **DATE OF BIRTH** 15/02/1990 | **NATIONALITY** FRENCH

Charles Pic was exposed to motor racing from an early age as his godfather is former F1 driver Éric Bernard. After a spell in French junior series, he moved into GP2 for 2010 and 2011, winning three races in the championship plus another in the GP2 Asia spin-off series. His performances impressed Marussia, who signed him to race in F1 in 2012 and he grabbed the headlines at the Belgian Grand Prix when he finished top in a free practice session, a rare feat for one of the smaller teams.

UNSUNG HEROES

"These are the unsung heroes of Formula 1.
So many people in the team do a great job – and an important job – but they work behind the garage or behind the scenes, away from the spotlight. It takes every person working together to make a team."

JAIME ALGUERSUARI

STATUS FORMER DRIVER | **DATE OF BIRTH** 23/03/1990 | **NATIONALITY** SPANISH

Jaime Alguersuari has impressed from an early age in motorsport. In 2008, he became the youngest ever winner of the prestigious British Formula Three title, beating challengers including Sergio Pérez. Less than a year later, he scored another first when he became the youngest driver ever to race in F1 by landing a drive with Toro Rosso, making him one of just seven teenagers to compete at the highest level of the sport. But motorsport isn't his only skill: Alguersuari is a successful DJ, whose debut album topped the iTunes electronic music chart, and he commentates on F1 for BBC Radio 5 Live.

THE ALHAMBRA PALACE

"My photo is of the Alhambra palace in Granada in southern Spain. It's a beautiful place. I *love* this amazing Andalusian spot, one of the most visited sights in the world."

57

MARIO ANDRETTI

STATUS 1978 WORLD CHAMPION | **DATE OF BIRTH** 28/02/1940 | **NATIONALITY** AMERICAN

Mario Andretti is one of motorsport's greatest all-rounders. As well as becoming Formula 1 world champion in 1978, he has also won the Indianapolis 500, the Daytona 500, four IndyCar titles and the International Race of Champions. In 2000, the year he retired from competition at the age of 60, Associated Press named him Driver of the Century. Since then he has focused on media work and running his winery in the Napa Valley.

FERRARI CLUB DAY AT THE ANDRETTI WINERY

"I took this amazing picture on April 17 2012, while there were 80 Ferraris parked at my winery in Napa Valley, California. I would have liked to get them all into the shot, but you get the idea! The Ferrari Club of America drives up the California coast to have lunch at Andretti Winery every year. They meet somewhere down south and drive up in a convoy – it's a spectacular sight. And when a tour bus arrives at the winery during the event and some visitors say 'I love your car collection, Mario', I just smile and say 'thank you'. If people think they're all mine… so be it!"

JOHN BOOTH

STATUS MARUSSIA TEAM PRINCIPAL | **DATE OF BIRTH** 18/12/1954 | **NATIONALITY** BRITISH

After a brief career racing junior single seaters, John Booth set up Manor Motorsport in 1990, initially to compete in Formula Renault. By 1999, the successful outfit had graduated to the British Formula Three Championship, where it won the title at its first attempt. Manor launched the careers of a host of F1 stars, including Lewis Hamilton, Kimi Räikkönen and Paul di Resta, and won its own entry into F1 in 2010, competing first as Virgin and then as Marussia.

YAS MARINA BY NIGHT

"For me, this is one of the most impressive sights we see on our Formula 1 world tour. There are important places for old and new on the calendar, but when Abu Dhabi did 'new', the result was simply breathtaking. This shot is of the Viceroy Hotel and it is the enduring image of the Abu Dhabi Grand Prix. My photography doesn't really do it justice."

ERIC BOULLIER

STATUS LOTUS TEAM PRINCIPAL | **DATE OF BIRTH** 09/11/1973 | **NATIONALITY** FRENCH

After graduating with a degree in aerospace engineering, Eric Boullier moved into motorsport with a job as chief engineer at the successful Spanish junior series outfit Racing Engineering. Before long he had been snapped up by French rival DAMS as its managing and technical director, where he ran France's entry in the A1GP World Cup of Motorsport. Boullier was also chief executive of young driver promoter Gravity Sport Management, and when Gravity's owners bought a stake in the Renault F1 team in 2009, Boullier was installed as team principal. The team has since changed its name to Lotus and with Boullier at the helm, has impressed many with its upturn in performance.

TUSCAN LANDSCAPE

"I took this picture in Tuscany a few years ago; the cypress trees lining the roads in the countryside are so typical of this beautiful region."

ROSS BRAWN

STATUS MERCEDES TEAM PRINCIPAL | **DATE OF BIRTH** 23/11/1954 | **NATIONALITY** BRITISH

Ross Brawn worked as an engineer for a number of teams, including Williams, before he was promoted to technical director at the Benetton team in 1991. There he was the driving force behind Michael Schumacher's world title successes in 1994 and 1995 and when Schumacher left for Ferrari in 1996, Brawn followed. There Schumacher won five more championships with Brawn's help, but when Schumacher retired Brawn was lured to Honda to become team principal for the first time. The team was off the pace and the car manufacturer quit in early 2009, leaving Brawn to save the team by buying it for just £1. Miraculously, under Brawn's guidance his eponymous team won both drivers' and constructors' world titles that year, with Mercedes stepping in as a new backer the following season.

THE PITS AT NIGHT

"The photo was taken at the 2011 Singapore Grand Prix from my seat on the pit wall as Michael Schumacher was pulling out of the garage during the second Friday practice session. As Formula 1's only night race, Singapore is such a unique event, and the lights in the pit lane and around the track make it a real spectacle for the fans. Hopefully this photo gives some idea of the atmosphere in the pit lane under lights."

SÉBASTIEN BUEMI

STATUS RED BULL RACING TEST DRIVER | **DATE OF BIRTH** 31/10/1988 | **NATIONALITY** SWISS

Being a Swiss racing driver is far from easy as the country has imposed a ban on motor racing since 1958. Sébastien Buemi has defied the odds, however, and joined F1 in 2009 with Toro Rosso after a successful career in junior racing series. He impressed from the start, scoring points on his debut, and followed that up with several more points-scoring finishes. He is now the test and reserve driver for world champions Red Bull Racing.

PARADISE ISLAND

"This picture was taken on Mauritius island. As everyone knows, the Formula 1 season is very long and I really like to take a little break somewhere very calm and relaxing after the season. I like this place very much because the weather and the beach are very good. I can really recover and when I fly back to Europe, I am full of energy."

67

KARUN CHANDHOK

STATUS FORMER DRIVER | **DATE OF BIRTH** 19/01/1984 | **NATIONALITY** INDIAN

Popular driver Karun Chandhok had a successful career in junior series, including GP2 and A1 Grand Prix, before making the break into F1 with HRT in 2010. He was reserve driver for Team Lotus in 2011, but is probably most fondly recognised among British fans for his knowledgeable and witty F1 commentary for BBC Radio 5 Live. In 2012 he entered the inaugural FIA World Endurance Championship and racked up an impressive sixth place in the Le Mans 24 Hours sportscar race at his first attempt.

ABU DHABI SUNSET

"I took a picture of this sunset over Yas Marina following the 2011 Abu Dhabi Grand Prix there. I think it looks simply stunning."

JÉRÔME D'AMBROSIO

STATUS LOTUS TEST DRIVER | **DATE OF BIRTH** 27/12/1985 | **NATIONALITY** BELGIAN

Jérôme d'Ambrosio got his first taste of F1 as test driver for the Renault and Virgin teams in 2010. He impressed and Virgin took him on as race driver for 2011. Despite driving a car which would finish last in the constructors' championship, he impressed with his reliability and managed to take three top-15 finishes during the year. He has since moved back to Renault, now renamed Lotus, as test driver and commentates for Sky Sports F1 in the UK and RTBF in Belgium.

THE WAITING GAME

"These are my former mechanics at Virgin waiting for a pit stop. They are always focused on the screens as they wait to take part in the action. It's always tense at any race, test or practice session."

71

STEFANO DOMENICALI

STATUS FERRARI TEAM PRINCIPAL | **DATE OF BIRTH** 11/05/1965 | **NATIONALITY** ITALIAN

Stefano Domenicali joined Ferrari straight from university, working in the car company's accounts department. Within a year he was given the chance to follow his love of motor racing when he became race director at Ferrari's Mugello circuit, where he organised events for series such as MotoGP and DTM. He fulfilled his dream in 1995 when he moved to the Ferrari F1 team and became team manager a year later. He rose steadily through the ranks until he was appointed team principal in 2008. Under his leadership, Ferrari claimed the 2008 constructors' world championship and has won races consistently since then.

FERNANDO ALONSO CYCLES BY

"Fernando is very, very good. We cannot ask for more. His level of competition is fantastic, like his attitude. He is flawless, accurate in working with his engineers and a reference for the whole team."

73

BERNIE ECCLESTONE

STATUS FORMULA ONE GROUP CHIEF EXECUTIVE | **DATE OF BIRTH** 28/10/1930 | **NATIONALITY** BRITISH

F1 supremo Bernie Ecclestone was involved in the sport long before the drivers – and many of the team principals – were born. After failed attempts to qualify for 1958 Monaco and British Grands Prix, he switched to driver management where he found the perfect outlet for his business skills. In 1972 he became owner of the Brabham team and got heavily involved in the complex political and financial negotiations that surrounded the sport. This culminated in 1981 with the signing of the first Concorde Agreement, the document which contracts the teams to race and sets out the division of the sport's revenues. This enabled Ecclestone to transform F1 into a world-class television spectacle and made him a billionaire in the process. He is now one of the world's richest men and is still at the helm of the sport he built up.

INTERESTING STATUES

"These two interesting statues are in my house in Gstaad in Switzerland. I can't remember where they came from but I like them a lot."

A CART FROM TURKEY

"This cart is outside my house in Gstaad. I think it came from somewhere like Turkey. It is just for decoration and not for use."

75

TONY FERNANDES

STATUS CATERHAM TEAM PRINCIPAL | **DATE OF BIRTH** 30/04/1964 | **NATIONALITY** MALAYSIAN

Tony Fernandes is one of the richest men in Malaysia with interests in airlines, hotels, financial services and telecoms, as well as the Caterham F1 Team and Queens Park Rangers football club. A big F1 fan, he first got involved in the sport when his AirAsia company sponsored Williams. In 2010 he entered F1 with his own team, then called Lotus but subsequently renamed Caterham after Fernandes' latest automotive investment. The outfit emerged as best of the three new teams in its opening season and was best of the three again in 2011.

CABIN CREW

"These members of the AirAsia cabin crew were our special guests at the 2011 Singapore Grand Prix and really brightened up the paddock! A welcoming smile is the best way to start any journey and being welcomed into the team garages by these four smiles was a great way to start the race weekend."

DAMON HILL

STATUS 1996 WORLD CHAMPION | **DATE OF BIRTH** 17/09/1960 | **NATIONALITY** BRITISH

Damon Hill is the only son of an F1 world champion to win the title himself. Following in his father Graham's footsteps, he took a well-earned victory in 1996 for Williams after finishing second in each of the two previous seasons. A fan favourite, he twice won the BBC Sports Personality of the Year award. He retired from F1 at the end of 1999 and is currently one of the presenters on Sky Sports F1, alongside overseeing the career of his son, aspiring F1 driver Josh.

SURFERS AT DUSK

"I'm a big fan of surfing and took this picture on a beach in Devon. After a day surfing, I was trying to capture the light on the dunes at dusk when some other surfers suddenly came running into the shot at exactly the right moment, making it the perfect photo opportunity."

CHRISTIAN HORNER

STATUS RED BULL RACING TEAM PRINCIPAL | **DATE OF BIRTH** 16/11/1973 | **NATIONALITY** BRITISH

Christian Horner started out in motorsport as a driver, but soon realised that he didn't have the speed necessary to make it all the way to the top. He decided instead to continue with Arden, the team he had set up to further his own career in Formula 3000, the forerunner to GP2. In 2003 and 2004, Arden won the F3000 championship and Horner's management skills caught the eye of Red Bull boss Dietrich Mateschitz, who had just bought out the Jaguar F1 team. He installed Horner as team principal of the new Red Bull Racing squad. The team struggled at first, but by 2009 it was a race winner and finished the season second in the championship. Horner then led the team to drivers' and constructors' world titles in both 2010 and 2011.

GOING FOR A DRIVE

"This picture is of the back of my Land Rover Defender, which our dogs love to ride around in. Hugo, the Airedale in the back, is particularly excited as you can see from his wagging tail, even though he doesn't know he's going for a haircut! Poppy, who is sitting in the front seat on the left, sadly died in January this year but we still have her two boys Bernie and Flavio, who get particularly car-sick… especially when my partner Beverley drives!"

VITANTONIO LIUZZI

STATUS FORMER DRIVER | **DATE OF BIRTH** 06/08/1981 | **NATIONALITY** ITALIAN

Vitantonio Liuzzi's bold driving style made him a favourite with many in the F1 paddock. He made his debut with Red Bull Racing in 2005, scoring a point on his first outing, before moving on to drives with Toro Rosso, Force India and HRT. Although never in a front running team, he impressed with plucky drives on a number of occasions, taking on some of the big names. Known for his sense of style, he now competes in the International Superstars Series touring car championship.

RACE KIT AND HELMET

"This photo is my helmet and race suit, clean, neat and tidy, waiting for me in the HRT motorhome before experiencing the drama of a Grand Prix."

83

VIJAY MALLYA

STATUS FORCE INDIA TEAM PRINCIPAL | **DATE OF BIRTH** 18/12/1955 | **NATIONALITY** INDIAN

Flamboyant Indian billionaire Vijay Mallya has been a fan of motorsport since childhood and became a Formula One team owner in 2007 when he bought the Spyker team, renaming it Force India. The team had hit on hard times and scored no points in 2008, finishing a lowly tenth in the championship. Under Mallya's leadership, the team slowly turned its fortunes around and by 2011 Force India finished the championship in sixth place, by far the best performance of the smaller teams. Away from the track, he collects artefacts associated with Indian history, including a Rolls-Royce refuse truck that once belonged to a maharajah.

BEFORE THE ITALIAN GRAND PRIX

"This photo was taken at Monza before Adrian Sutil went to the grid for the 2011 Italian Grand Prix. It shows the activity in the garage as the anticipation builds ahead of the race."

ADRIAN NEWEY

STATUS RED BULL RACING CHIEF TECHNICAL OFFICER | **DATE OF BIRTH** 26/12/1958 | **NATIONALITY** BRITISH

Adrian Newey is widely recognised as one of the greatest designers in the history of Formula 1. He first came to the attention of the racing world when, at the age of just 25, he designed the car which won the 1984 Indianapolis 500. After more race victories and two CART championships, he returned to Europe and where his designs for the Leyton House F1 team caught the attention of Williams, who hired him in 1990. His cars powered the team to five constructors' championships and four drivers' titles before he quit for McLaren, where his car won both titles in 1998. He joined Red Bull Racing in 2006 with the aim of turning around the fortunes of the struggling new team. This was realised when his cars won both championships in 2010 and 2011.

TRACTOR IN RAJASTHAN

"This picture was taken in India last year when I took some holiday with my family after the Indian Grand Prix and travelled around. Towards the end of the trip we stayed in a wilderness camp in Rajasthan and toured some of the surrounding villages. Life there is humble with simple homes and no televisions. The people are happy and friendly but have a tough existence living off the land. I thought this tractor epitomised those characteristics."

LUIS PÉREZ-SALA

STATUS HRT TEAM PRINCIPAL | **DATE OF BIRTH** 15/05/1959 | **NATIONALITY** SPANISH

Luis Pérez-Sala made his name as an F1 driver before becoming a team principal. He raced for Minardi in the 1980s, scoring a sixth-place finish at the 1989 British Grand Prix before going on to win the Spanish touring car championship twice. After retiring from driving, he continued to work in motorsport, running the Circuit de Catalunya's young driver programme. He was appointed by HRT as an advisor in 2011 before being promoted to team principal in 2012.

IN THE PITS

"I've been linked with competition all my life and forming a part of this F1 project is something very special and unique. The start wasn't easy but seeing what we've achieved in such little time makes me feel tremendously proud of this team. This photo reflects a small part of the work done and those who have made it possible. That's what it says to me: hard work, pride and a desire to improve."

89

PETER SAUBER

STATUS SAUBER TEAM PRINCIPAL | **DATE OF BIRTH** 13/10/1943 | **NATIONALITY** SWISS

Peter Sauber built his first racing car in his parents' basement. It was a success and launched his career as a team owner. He worked his way up through various sportscar championships until a partnership with Mercedes in the late 1980s helped his cars finish first and second in the 1989 Le Mans 24 Hours and the 1989 and 1990 World Sportscar manufacturers' and drivers' championships. Sauber had his sights on F1 and his eponymous team made its debut in 1993. It was moderately successful and in 2001 finished fourth in the constructors' championship, beating several better-funded teams. Sauber sold a majority stake to BMW in 2006 and it was under this partnership that the team won its first race at the Canadian Grand Prix in 2008 with Robert Kubica at the wheel. Sauber bought the team back in 2009 and remains team principal.

VIEW FROM THE LIVING ROOM WINDOW

"This is one of my favourite views in the world. I took this photo from the living room of my weekend cottage in Switzerland, which is located in the Kanton Graubünden (which is also known as Canton Grisons). The mountains are called the Signina group."

ADRIAN SUTIL

STATUS FORMER DRIVER | **DATE OF BIRTH** 11/01/1983 | **NATIONALITY** GERMAN

Adrian Sutil made his Formula One debut in 2007 for the Spyker team and scored the only point of the team's brief F1 career at the Japanese Grand Prix. By the end of the year it had been bought out by Indian billionaire Vijay Mallya and renamed Force India, but Sutil stayed on. Points were hard to come by at first, but at the 2009 Italian Grand Prix, Sutil scored a stunning fourth place, setting the fastest lap in the process. More strong points finishes followed in 2010 and 2011.

MY VIEW WHEN I RACE

"The picture was taken in the pit garage at Monza. It was my cockpit and working place for the last five years. That's the view I have when I race, and you can see how low it is."

FRANZ TOST

TEAM TORO ROSSO TEAM PRINCIPAL | **DATE OF BIRTH** 20/01/1956 | **NATIONALITY** AUSTRIAN

Franz Tost's first foray into motorsport was as a driver, but although he was quick enough to win the 1983 Austrian Formula Ford Championship, he never felt he would reach the top as a driver and took a sports management degree instead. He used his knowledge to get various jobs in motor racing and got his first taste of F1 working for the management team of Ralf Schumacher. He also looked after the driver's interests at Jordan and Williams, before becoming the operations manager of BMW's F1 programme. When Toro Rosso was launched in 2006 he was appointed team principal and has managed the team ever since, inspiring it to victory in the 2008 Italian Grand Prix.

THE STARS OF THE SHOW

"Formula 1 is a team sport using high-tech machinery but in the end, what people remember over the years apart from a handful of truly beautiful racing cars, are the drivers. They are the stars of the show, the centre of attention and the ones who bring the racing to life on Sunday afternoons. So here is our current line-up of youngsters, Daniel Ricciardo and Jean-Eric Vergne, full of talent and full of hope for the future."

JARNO TRULLI

STATUS FORMER DRIVER | **DATE OF BIRTH** 13/07/1974 | **NATIONALITY** ITALIAN

Jarno Trulli enjoyed a long and successful F1 career, driving for a host of big-name teams including Renault, Jordan, Toyota and Lotus. Between 1997 and 2011 he started 252 races and appeared on the podium 11 times, but his career highlight was taking victory for Renault from pole position at the 2004 Monaco Grand Prix. He joined Lotus in 2010 and brought an experienced pair of hands to the newcomer, leading the team for two years before retiring from F1 at the end of 2011.

WAITING FOR THE DRIVERS' PARADE

"I took this photo before the pre-race driver parade at the first Indian Grand Prix in October 2011. It's the only time when all the drivers are together."

MURRAY WALKER

STATUS FORMER COMMENTATOR | **DATE OF BIRTH** 10/10/1923 | **NATIONALITY** BRITISH

Murray Walker is one of the most famous and best-loved voices in British sport. His first taste of motorsport came at an early age thanks to his motorcycle racer father Graham. Alongside a career in advertising – which included creating the slogan 'Trill makes budgies bounce with health' – Walker began commentating on motor races in 1948, but it wasn't until the 1970s that the BBC began to show regular coverage of Formula 1. Walker was the obvious choice as lead commentator, but it was in the 1980s that he really became a household name when his friction with co-commentator and former world champion James Hunt helped make F1 compulsive viewing. Famous for his enthusiastic delivery and a tendency to make well-intended errors in the heat of the moment, he retired from live Grand Prix commentary at the age of 78 after the 2001 United States GP.

A RARE VINTAGE

"My photo features a very rare four-cylinder AJS of 1931 vintage, which I took at the Graham Walker Memorial Run at the National Motor Museum, Beaulieu in August 2012. The event is held every year to honour my father, who died 50 years ago."

MARTIN WHITMARSH

STATUS McLAREN TEAM PRINCIPAL | **DATE OF BIRTH** 29/04/1958 | **NATIONALITY** BRITISH

Unlike most of his contemporaries, Martin Whitmarsh worked outside motorsport for several years before coming into F1. He was manufacturing director at British Aerospace, in charge of Hawk and Harrier airframe production, before he moved to McLaren as head of operations in 1989. In 1997 he was promoted to managing director at the team and held several senior positions before he became team principal in 2009 following the retirement of Ron Dennis. Under Whitmarsh's leadership, the team has stayed on winning form.

VIEW FROM THE PIT WALL

"This is very representative of the view from the pit wall during a Grand Prix weekend. Being up on the pit wall gives you a good look into both garages – you can very quickly work out what's happening and whether things are going well or not. It also gives you clear sight up and down the pit lane, so you can judge what your competitors are up to. Compositionally, I thought it was interesting to split the image in half, filling the top half with flat panelling, and the lower half with all the action in the F1 garage. I might not be David Bailey, but I have a go!"

SIR FRANK WILLIAMS

TEAM WILLIAMS TEAM PRINCIPAL | **DATE OF BIRTH** 16/04/1942 | **NATIONALITY** BRITISH

Sir Frank Williams is one of the most successful team principals in Formula 1 history. He founded the Williams F1 team in 1977 and since then has spearheaded nine constructors' and seven drivers' championships, for Alan Jones (1980), Keke Rosberg (1982), Nelson Piquet (1987), Nigel Mansell (1992), Alain Prost (1993), Damon Hill (1996) and Jacques Villeneuve (1997). The team recently returned to winning form after eight years in the wilderness when Pastor Maldonado took a surprise victory in the 2012 Spanish Grand Prix.

MESSAGE IN THE SAND IN QATAR

"This picture was taken whilst I was visiting Doha, Qatar. Williams has a research and development facility there called the Williams Technology Centre, and I was visiting to take a look at the progress being made and visit local dignitaries. Williams F1 and the Middle East have a long association – our first-ever sponsors were from the region, so it has a special significance for our organisation. The weather's not bad either!"

CHAMPAGNE MOMENT
Red Bull Racing driver
Mark Webber celebrates
in style after overhauling
Fernando Alonso in the
closing stages to win the
2012 British Grand Prix at
Silverstone.